The Red Sea
is
Your Blood

"A lifetime devoted unremittingly to the study of the ancient backgrounds of our modern Western religion has established beyond all possibility of error the conviction that the great Scriptures of antiquity on which our Occidental faiths have been built up have had a remote Egyptian origin. The present treatise is an attempt to justify the truth of this statement by the revelation of the recondite significance covertly adumbrated in one of the most prominent of such archaic symbols found in the Bibles of both Judaism and Christianity,—the Red Sea. Studied through the lens of a larger vision and a deeper understanding, it should, and eventually will be seen, to release the power of a new and far more vital message for the two religions that have harbored, all unsuspectingly, the hidden dynamic of this archaic construction of semantic genius. This revelation of the cryptic significance of the Red Sea in its Bible usage could inaugurate another, and the most thoroughgoing, reformation in Judaism and Christianity since the ancient days of their origin. It could engender a New Enlightenment in the life of religion and spiritual culture not only in the West, but in the world at large."

Alvin Boyd Kuhn

ISBN 1-56459-328-2

A lifetime devoted unremittingly to the study of the ancient backgrounds of our modern Western religion has established beyond all possibility of error the conviction that the great Scriptures of antiquity on which our Occidental faiths have been built up have had a remote Egyptian origin and that they purveyed their profound message of truth and wisdom in a language of semantic crypticism that has first baffled, then deluded the minds of all the theological savants, both Jewish and Christian, who have endeavored to interpret their esoteric significance, for full two thousand years. The present treatise is an attempt to justify the truth of this statement by the revelation of the recondite significance covertly adumbrated in one of the most prominent of such archaic symbols found in the Bibles of both Judaism and Christianity, — the RED SEA. At the moment of publication it is believed that never in all the centuries since the days of Egypt's ancient glory has this occult meaning, involving, as it does, the stake of the historicity of the Old Testament, with repercussions even for the narrative of the New Testament, been known or published. It may therefore rightly lay claim to being certainly one of the most significant revelations in the area of religious intelligence in twenty centuries at least. Almost alone in its single power of truth it threatens to subvert the main theological supports of Judaism first and then Christianity. Such at first sight would seem to be the effect of the tremendous implications of its disclosure at the present epoch in world religion, particularly in Judaism and Christianity. This, however, would represent a narrow and myopic view of its significance. Studied through the lens of a larger vision and a deeper understanding, it should, and eventually will be seen, to release the power of a new and far more vital message for the two religions that have harbored, all unsuspectingly, the hidden dynamic of this archaic construction of semantic genius. This revelation of the cryptic significance of the Red Sea in its Bible usage could inaugurate another, and the most thoroughgoing, reformation in Judaism and Christianity since the ancient days of their origin. It could engender a New Enlightenment in the life of religion and spiritual culture not only in the West, but in the world at large.

The arcane profundity of the divine wisdom vouchsafed to early humanity by gods or at least by sages and seers of advanced human development, "holy men of old," as the Scriptures themselves rate them, was considered to be a treasure fit only to be preserved in a casket constructed of the golden material of transcendent imagery and jewelled with gems of the sublimest and most majestic symbolism. Minds open to the vision of its truth and beauty designed that it be expressed in recondite forms and semantic devices, which, while they obscured its purport for the immature and undeveloped masses, intimated its dynamic significance and released its cathartic power to the intelligent and the initiated. These devices were such literary "genres" as allegory, myth, drama, poetry, legend, epic fiction, imaginative tropes, number structures, star groupings and movements, and above all, nature symbols. The outer world of nature, which the seers knew to be the language of God's own expression of true being and which lay concreted before our eyes, was looked to for all the expressive types needed to body forth the archetypes of eternal verity. Nature spoke the one language which could never utter falsehood. Hence the sacred literature abounds in naturographs, with such elementary natural objects employed to dramatize meaning as the tree, grass, earth, sky, water, air, fire, the stream, animal, bird, insect, reptile, stone, wood, metal, storm, wave, tide, rain, snow, desert, mountain, flower, bee, grape — and the great sea. These natural objects and the phenomena of their living existence constituted a veritable language, and one need not hesitate to pronounce it the most completely meaningful language available to man. It is the tragedy of world culture that this semantic idiom has, like Latin, ancient Greek and other tongues, become a "dead language" and the books written in it stand as tomes of fast sealed mystery. As a result the whole enterprise of theology and Scriptural interpretation has, for centuries, been befogged in intellectual confusion.

It is the purpose to deal in this essay with just one of the nature symbols that has found such general use in the Bibles of antiquity, and the attempt will be made to bring to light the pure gold of meaning esoterically hidden in its cryptic intimations. There is said to be gold in the chemical composition of sea water; it is possible to say that there is also intellectual gold of precious truth in what sea water was intended to present to thought in the Scriptures. It is believed that one is fully warranted in prefacing the effort with the observation that the revelation here to be made constitutes one of the most astounding disclosures of occult knowledge to be found in all the realm of the archaic religious literature of the world. The Red Sea.

In the very same century in which Christianity took its rise, in fact born almost in the same year as that claimed for the birth of Jesus of Nazareth, lived the Hebrew scholar and philosopher, Philo Judaeus. The statement will hardly be contradicted now that he had formulated a systematic code of interpretation of ancient sacred writings, which, if it had been followed closely by scriptural exegetists, would have saved the science of theology from the confusion into which it has fallen ever since his day. It might even have prevented the schism between Judaism and its ungrateful daughter, Christianity, which was destined to drench the pages of two thousand years of religious history with needless rivers of blood. It would likewise have obviated the causes which led both religions to break up into numberless sects and denominations, thus perpetuating the reign of sullen hatreds and bigotries of every sort.

He elucidated the principle that the tomes of sacred writing bequeathed to early humanity by the gods or by men of far advanced evolutionary stature were susceptible of interpretation at four different levels of understanding: (1) the literal-physical; (2) the moral-sentimental; (3) the allegorical-intellectual; (4) the anagogical-mystical. That is, the books of Holy Writ could be read as historical events; as moral instruction; as intellectual conception of truth; as the incitement to the most exalted spiritual mystical transports. Even before Philo's day the great and learned Jewish scholars and interpreters of the Torah, the Tanaim and Amoraim, had expounded the principle that he who reads the Scriptures only at the level of their surface meaning will never grasp the truth of the living Word of God, that only he who pierces the coarser veils to grasp a far deeper sense and experience a more vivid illumination of consciousness will receive the cathartic purification of his nature. They went so far as to say that he who was content with the surface meaning of the words was a fool and a simpleton. As long as religions cling to the lower rungs of the scale of interpretation of their Scriptures, there will be endless points of difference between them; if they will lift the sense to the upper third and fourth levels, the apparent outer grounds of difference will dissolve in the unity and harmony of a lofty conceptual enlightenment. The later philosophers Kant and Spinoza were to arrive at about this same basis of understanding. Philo himself so well succeeded in elucidating Scriptural meaning at the highest level that he was able to make a synthesis of the Hebrew Pentateuch, or first five books of the Old Testament, with the rationalistic systematism of the Platonic philosophy of the Greeks. It can with a great degree of plausibility be asserted that had his interpretative achievement been used as the basis of Biblical exegesis from that time, the catastrophic divergence of Christianity from its parent Judaism would have been avoided, and the world spared the gruesome horrors of two thousand years of persecution and slaughter.

The key and instrument for apprehension of the more exalted sense of Scripture was of course the *allegorical* approach to understanding. When one understands that one is reading a volume of spiritual truth expressed in the guise of allegories, one looks beyond or beneath the common connotation of the words to discern a transcendental significance that can be apprehended only mystically, or at least with the power of abstract conception. In the late second and early third centuries the two great Christian expositors of Scripture, Clement and Origen, successive heads of the leading academy of Christian doctrinism, the famous school of Alexandria, endeavored valiantly to exalt the principles of Biblical exegesis to the highest Philonic level. Every historian of Christianity has had to devote a chapter or section of his work to an exposition of what is spoken of as "Origen's allegories." To the detriment of all Christian history the historians almost with one accord, belittle the importance and significance of this chapter of the early life of the faith. On the contrary, it will some day be seen that the religion's failure to cultivate and perpetuate and further develop the methodology employed by these two great Fathers has been the saddest dereliction and most costly fatality of Christian history.

THE RETURN TO ALLEGORY

It is evident now that a keen recognition of this unfortunate eventuality in the early development of Christianity has taken place quite recently in the Roman Catholic branch of the Christian establishment. The hierarchy of this great ecclesiastical system has obviously arrived at the decision to open the doors of Bible study to the allegorical approach and method for interpretation. Recent public utterances have voiced the policy of the Church of Rome that, since the Bible authors resorted to a wide variety of "literary forms," such as allegory, myth, drama and symbol, readers are free now to put their own interpretation upon the textual material. Allegory is bound in the end to convey to each reader the special sense which each is able to grasp, hence the attempt to confine the meaning to a stated and uniform exposition is futile at best. This move leaves every one at liberty to extract from the reading of Scripture the particular grade of conception of which each is capable.

Few realize the epochal significance of this strategy of the Catholic Church. It is a virtual confession that it was a mistake to have failed to follow the lead of Philo, Clement and Origen. The deeper meaning of the great Scriptures is after all only to be caught by each reader in proportion to his receptive capabilities in the way of spiritual-mystical realization. The pressures impingeing upon intelligence today from the side of a more enlightened scholarship have made this recognition and concession necessary. To contend any longer that the Bible is to be taken with Fundamentalist literalism, and as in all parts factual history, would leave Catholicism stranded high and dry on the banks, while the stream of a more intelligent, more meaningful and dynamic Scriptural exegesis has swept on by, carrying the world of culture with it out of reach of the old method. Lately, too, the trend back to allegorism has manifested itself sensationally in the Protestant wing of Christianity, especially in the Episcopalian denomination.

As this essay is to reveal a series of astounding items of lost knowledge, it might as well detonate its most explosive datum right at the start, with the positive declaration that *the Red Sea is not now and never was in the Bible!* This is folly! This is crazy! One can hear readers protest. Yet the statement means exactly what it asserts, and it is true! Any one can pick up an English Bible and point to the words: R-e-d S-e-a. But if one picks up and opens a Moffatt translation of the Bible, those words will *not* be found in it, for this learned translator had the intelligence and the courage to take those two words out. Because he knew that they never had a right to be there! And all other learned scholars knew that they had no right to be there, yet suffered them to remain. No modern translation has a right to inject into its version something the equivalent of which never was found in the original document. And no original ancient edition of the Bible ever contained the Hebrew equivalent of the English words "Red Sea." But the original Hebrew editions did contain two words which translators, or some translator at some given period, found reasons for translating into English as the "Red Sea."

The interested reader is by now probably eager to know what those two Hebrew words are. It is no secret; here they are: *Iam suph*. *Iam*, sure enough, means water, sea; but *suph* never meant "red." On the contrary it means something decidedly *green*. Any Hebrew dictionary carries the information that *suph* means *sedge, marsh grass, swamp grass*, in short, *reeds! Iam suph* then means the Reedy Sea, Sea of Reeds, the Reed Sea! And ancient Egyptian literature did call it the "Great Green Sea." We shall see how it became red.

Suddenly, then, we are faced with the realization, quite staggering to all in the aura of what we were told in Sabbath Schools or read in Bible treatises, that no Bible ever said that the children of Israel once crossed — two and a quarter million in one night — the geographical and very wet Red Sea lying between Egypt and Arabia on the map of our physical globe. If that Red Sea is not even so much as mentioned in the Bible narrative, how can it be asserted that these people crossed it, wet or dry? And what then, we dazedly begin to speculate, becomes of the whole epic of the Israelites in Egypt and their miraculous midnight flight out of it?

It is to be interjected here — since the suspense may be irritating — that, true enough, the hosts of the true Israelites (when one knows who they really were) did cross the Red Sea (when one knows *what that truly is*), and the story comes alive with tenfold more luminous significance than the alleged physical miracle of passing across between two walls of water ever meant or could mean. For, as now we are staggered by the wiping away of the meaning we had attributed to the thing as presumed history, we can be even more happily staggered by the revelation of a veritable radiance of sublime significance which, as spiritual allegory, it was certainly designed to convey to minds attuned to logical reasoning and mystical apperceptions.

But now that we have washed the "Red Sea" completely out of the story, and put in its place the "Reed Sea," we are — momentarily — more "at sea" than ever as to what this green sea can mean. Where is it located? What is the hidden significance of the Israelites crossing it to escape from Egypt's reluctant Pharaoh?

Pff! — the orthodox, the Fundamentalist scholars will exclaim — why make all this exaggerated fuss about a mere change of name? We should not let a little quirk of literary usage like that disturb us or shake our faith in the Scripture. The narrow section of the real geographical Red Sea, where the Israelites picked their passage, was a place of low water and reedy character, and the Bible says that the Lord raised up an "east wind" that pushed the shallow water off the bottom, so that the people crossed while the wind held the water back. To a Fundamentalist nature's laws and elements present no obstacle to belief when God is working a "miracle." Therefore it means nothing to him to reflect that if an *east* wind blew the shallow water off the bottom, it would pile it all upon the *west* shore of the channel, exactly where the Israelites would have to start their crossing! Nor does he pause to take into account the inches of mud on the bottom. Even with a modern highway across the strait, and equipped with all modern vehicles, an army of trained men of that number could not cross the Red Sea in a week. Imagine over a million women, children, camp followers, flocks and herds, making the crossing in one night! In too many circles in religion it is still considered a sacrilege to let natural law stand in the way of a divine miracle. If God has staged a wonder and prodigy of his arbitrary power, it is for humanity to stand agape.

The next startling disclosure in the context must wait until sufficient preliminary elucidation had been made to render it intelligible. An allegory — at any rate ancient Scriptural allegory — was a literary device designed to pictorialize a spiritual or anagogical reality in man's subjective experience in the form of an earthly physical narrative of fictitious events. So we are quite warranted, without further demonstration, in assuming that the story of this crossing is designed to carry its meaning into the area of our subjective life to work there a proper "miracle" of understanding at the two higher levels of Philo's scale. As to this it can be said at once that virtually all Scriptural allegories and other semantic modes of representing exalted truth and noumenal realities have but one basic theme to dilate upon — the incarnation of souls in mortal bodies here on earth. That is the ubiquitous omnipresent theme at the heart of nearly all Biblical writing. This basic event, the essence of human life itself, is treated, enlivened, illuminated by a great variety of imaginative constructions, and this is possible because all living forms manifest the basic principle from one angle or another and can be dramatized by one typology or another. Life everywhere speaks the same language and harps upon the same chords.

This Red Sea episode of the sacred allegory was formulated in order to transfix the more capable human conceptual faculty with the reality of the spiritual fact that the divine seed-soul, a unit of God's mind-generated being, a true Son of the Father, had in incarnation to escape from a bondage to the lower nature of the animal body in which it was housed for its journey through this mortal life, by crossing a place, state or condition of existence symbolized most fittingly by a body of water. This typism is found universally in the arcane wisdom literature. Very many instances of it could be cited, — and have been in our other works. If one says that in life after life, or in the complete cycle of incarnate life, the soul has to wade through the "sea of life" eventually to land on that "farther shore" of celestial delight and radiance, the poetic figure sinks deeply enough into the average mind to register the general sense of the incarnation experience. If, however, the language of symbolism had been continuously cultivated since ancient days the figure would release upon consciousness the vivid force of its real significance.

But it must be forcefully asserted at this point that those sages of old who indited our sacred Scriptures were not merely indulging wayward fancy in light touches of poetic imagery. Artists they were of the highest genius and adept in the faculty of analogical representation as none others have perhaps been since their day. Every image they conceived to pictorialize metaphysical verity was a construction that carried the receptive mind into the heart of a living truth and impressed it upon reflection with the dynamic of what the Greeks called a spiritual catharsis. In the Platonic philosophy these poetic figures stood as archetypes of the divine thought, and deep reflection upon them awakened realizations of the mighty transfiguring power of noumenal truth that is the very bread of life for man's soul.

The sagacious scribes of the archaic wisdom, then, were talking of a sea which all souls must cross, and cross without sinking too deep in its waters; in fact a sea on whose surface we must learn to walk without sinking, or getting our feet enmired in the mud of its bottom; a sea again whose waters must figuratively be dried up by the power of God so that we may pass over on dry land. Or perhaps, under a variant figure, a great fish might catch us up and transport us across after a three days' journey in its "cabin." Is all this just light poetic fancy, or is there in truth and in fact such a sea that we must cross to escape a miserable slavery and reach a delectable land flowing with milk and honey? Is the soul actually brought in contact with real water that might extinguish its divine fire and drown it?

AN OCEAN ON FIRE

It is next to inconceivable how blind the intellect of a world has been! How obtuse to a reality that the allegory pressed upon it in the plainest terms! So close to us is this red sea over whose storm-tossed billows we must swim to reach a happier land that it could not be brought any closer to us.

> Closer is he than breathing,
> Nearer than hands and feet,—

sang the poet Tennyson of the divine Self within us. And just as close to us is this very red sea of life. For, far down into the depths of an actual body of water, incarnation has plunged these souls of ours that are as oblivious of the watery element they swim in as they are of the air they breathe. So true is this, both as allegory and as fact, that ancient poetic genius typified the soul as a great fish swimming about in the sea, the soul of life immersed in water. Early Christianity still carried this symbol, as both Augustine and Tertullian said that the Christ was the great fish in the sea and his Christian followers were the little minnows. The fish, as symbol of divinity, was universal in the arcane typology and in mythology. And when souls had descended into incarnation they were aptly likened unto fish in the sea. In actuality, souls are immersed in a vessel of living potential *that is seven-eighths water,* and it *is* sea water! And, open a vein and let it out and the oxygen immediately turns it red! The Red Sea!

At last the astounding truth strikes home to the mind of a surprised world: this "Red Sea" which all Sons of God, the only "Israelites" ever spoken of in the Holy Scriptures, have to cross — is the human body blood! With a clear, sharp sense of understanding will any deep-thinking mind now realize the dynamic force and literal truth adumbrated by the allegorical figure of our souls having to sink down in, wade through, swim across or be transported over a body of water, which on the side of a poetic figure, the Reed Sea, is green, but on the side of physical reality is actually red. Every life of eighty years entails an immersion of the fiery element of soul in these bodies of water and crossing them to the farther shore. Eventually, in the war between the fire of soul and the water of body, which incarnation precipitates, the unquenchable fire of soul must dry up the "moist elements" and permit the soul to cross without "getting its feet wet." So we have the beauty of the divine parable which could not be caught as long as allegory was mistaken for alleged Jewish history, most of which, if it is looked at closely and realistically as presumed actual event, is seen as preposterous and impossible.

If a skeptical reader insists upon challenging the truth of the declaration that the human body blood is sea water, and not only in poetry but in chemical constituency, the authority back of the statement is that of science, of biology, of anthropology, of evolution, of chemical analysis verified in the laboratory. The human blood *is* ocean water, declared so by chemistry, salinity and all, so that analysis can find no essential character difference between the two. One could logically infer this fact even without verification by chemical analysis, from a basic knowledge that the stream of biological life in its evolution came originally out of the oceans. For a long, early period confined to the sea, it later became transferred to the land; the sustenance of bodily energy through the chemical properties of water was replaced by the elements in air; gills were exchanged for lungs. Yet, the lymphs, plasms and humors in the organisms retained the primal character of what they had been from the start, — sea water. The action of oxygen on substances tends to give them a red coloration. Indeed we do retain the original heritage of the sea in our veins. Our blood is this "Red Sea." The ocean is our common mother; and half of the goddesses of mythology and the Scriptures actually perpetuate their identity with the sea in their names, most prominently Thallath (Greek word for "sea") and Mary (Latin for "sea," *Maria*).

Language is the deep mine of occult meaning which must be worked constantly if one is to bring up the precious ore of living truth in the arcane science of old. If the writers of the Hebrew Old Testament had wanted to speak of the Red Sea explicitly, instead of the *iam suph*, they would have written *iam adom*, for "red" in Hebrew is *adom*. The Hebrew word for "blood" is *dam*. *Adam'dam* means "reddish," *admoni* means "red-haired." The word for "ground, earth" is *adamah*; hence, as *adam* is the word for "man," but was included in the word *adamah*, meaning "ground, earth," the name Adam was given the meaning of "red earth." And in one way that is exactly what man is, his earthy body mixed with red blood. By a mere switch of vowels, *adam* became Edom, and Edom is the patronymic of Esau, who was "red, hairy." We find that connection of *Edom* with *red* in the first verses of the 63rd chapter of *Isaiah*: "Who is this that comes from Edom, with his garments dyed *red* from Bozrah? Wherefore art thou *red* in thine apparel, and thy garments like him that treadeth in the winefat?"

But this is only the beginning of what etymology, philology can do for us in this green-red symbolism. It is no wonder, incidentally in passing, that green and red are the two colors typical of the Christmas season and its symbolism, as green stands for the natural man, and red, as the color of fire, typifies the spiritual man, and it is the ultimate marriage of these two components in man's nature that gives birth to the Christ consciousness.

Back there in ancient Egypt we come upon another precious nugget of language revelation. In fact it becomes the basis of the gist of this treatise. We find there the origin of the word "sea" itself, a most illuminating item of knowledge.

The fundamental predication of the great Egyptian wisdom structure was the interaction of the two polarized energies of spirit and matter, on a web of force suspended between which the axis of the universe is conceived as turning. The Egyptian spiritual or cosmogonic mythology traced the generation of the two universal creative energies of life in a semantic structure which said that the God Tum (in one version, Kepher in another) with his hand produced from his generative power his seminal seed, "and from the drops of *blood* which fell upon the earth, were born the gods Hu and Sa" (in another version Shu and Tefnut). And these twins, god and goddess, brother and sister, Hu and Sa, became the progenitors of mankind. These two short names stood to the Egyptian seers as Hu for spirit, and Sa for matter. And as *fire* was the universal symbol of spirit, so *water*, its chemical antagonist, was the symbol of matter. This gives us the association of the word *sa* with water. But in the Egyptian system of hieroglyphics the tonal symbol of fire was the letter of the alphabet, *sh*. The evidence of this, beside many other items, is that the Hebrew word for *fire* is *esh*. As the unit of conscious being, what would be the ego-consciousness, or I-consciousness, was alphabetically embodied in the capital letter "I," and this self-consciousness was embodied, as far as this earth is concerned, in the creature *man*, the Hebrew word for "man" combined the "I" of divine consciousness with the "sh" of fire, so that "man" in Hebrew is *ish*. As "Hu" was the unit of spiritual life, man thus became the *Hu*-man being. And since this *Hu*man entity tenants a body of water, we have a suggestive ground for the words *hu*mid, *hu*midity and the "*humors*" of the body. We shall now look at the words derived from the *Sa* stem and shall find them interesting and illuminating indeed.

Immediately it seems indubitable that we have here the true origin of the word "sea" itself. Since Sa was matter, and water its symbol, the great water mass on the earth was the *s(e)a*. Possibly some one introduced the "e" into the Sa to hide its derivation from the latter, in the esoteric spirit which motivated all ancient religious literature. This ruse was often resorted to, the "Red Sea" itself being an instance of it.

But what is that element in the composition of sea water that is most directly associated with it? *Salt*, of course! And salt is *sodium chloride*, no less. Sa, sea, salt!

And salt is used as a *preservative*. In man's constitution, say all the great Scriptures, is an element, a divine principle, that is described as the "salt of the earth," and hence is that which *saves* man and is the rock of his *salvation*. So we have the words *save, safe, salvation, salvage,* (probably) *saliva, sane, salud* (Spanish word for "health"), *salute, salad, salubrious, salutary, salacious,* and by a poetic stretch, *sail* (over the bounding main, as the old school song has it), and others. As *salute* is to *hail, sail* equates *hail,* and in fact "s" and "h" interchange places between words in different languages or even in the same language thousands of times, as in the Hindu Asura and the Persian Ahura. It is quite a likely fact that the presence of salt in the world oceans maintains chemically a balance between elements that keeps the world atmosphere "salubrious." All the muck of the continents is carried by rivers into the briny deep, and it is that saline component of our seas that preserves the purity of our air, one must suppose. So then. if *salud* (health) and *salute* (generally an inquiry about a person's *health*), and *sail* and *hail* are kindred in original meaning, we have at once a connection of *hail* with *hale,* and also with *heal* and the German *heil (hail)* and *heilig,* "sacred, holy". Doubtless this chain extends further.

At least two allegorical constructions in the Bible introduce this element of salt and they now become most significant. Could it be pure "coincidence" that the strange incident of the turning of Lot's wife into that pillar of salt (which Josephus said was still standing in his day, the first century A.D.!) occurred at a city called Sodom? Here the hint thrown out above comes in for consideration. Are we stretching things too far if we identify Sodom with sodium(chloride)? When it is remembered that in the ancient Hebrew manuscripts and the original Egyptian scripts back of them vowels were few and virtually nondescript and almost indistinguishable, there is nothing authoritatively to be introduced against the identity. (Vowels only later in the Greek came to distinctness, and the Greek has the full complement of seven.) If, in passing, the question of the esoteric significance of the pillar-of-salt allegory is raised, perhaps the interpretation is that if on the soul's "fleeing" from the condition of embodiment in bodies composed mainly of sea-salt water, it does not continue straight ahead in its evolution toward spiritual heights, but turns to look back and seek again the attractions of life of body, it will be drawn back for further incarnations in salty bodies, the body being poetized as this pillar of salt. If this is not the significance, the real meaning must lie much deeper indeed.)

Then in the fourteenth chapter of *Genesis* the first verses tell of a battle between five kings on one side and four on the other, waged in "the vale of *Siddim*, which is the *salt sea*." (Another version has it, "at the salt marshes," — the Reed Sea.) Not only do we have Sodom connected with the salt sea, but now Siddim, and vowels not to be considered of any decisive importance. Nor does the doubling of the "d" make any difference, as consonants were constantly being doubled, according to certain euphonic principles. Sodium, Sodom, Siddim, and all very saline!

Can one be simply in error in affirming, then, that all these allegorical flourishes are ancient semantic devices hiding in their cryptic methodology the flat meaning that the great battle of life, the war between the carnal and the spiritual elements in man's nature, is fought out right here in the sodium chloride in the blood of these bodies of ours? There is, indeed, reinforcement for the idea in the Bible's repeated statement that "in the blood is the life of the soul." A piquant phrase of universal usage in referring to strong character and sterling quality as being in a person's blood, is seen to have a basis here.

And ancient Egypt speaks up in this connection, too. In referring to the universal duality of spirit and matter, it poetizes the two polar energies as the Pool of the Sun and the Pool of the Moon; the Pool of the North and the Pool of the South; and again the Pool of *Natron* and the Pool of Salt. This natron is intriguing; for it starts with *na-*, and the chemical formula for salt is NA-CL. Obviously the *na* is for sodium. Chemistry might tell us of some connection here that would again assure us that these ancient Egyptians knew more occult truth than we have ever given them credit for. Some one could tell us more about natron and its properties. *Na-* is significant as beginning both "nature" and "name," and, oddly enough, in Scriptural usage, name and nature were close to identical in meaning. The patriarchs always called upon the *name* of the Lord. One's name was an intrinsic part of one's identity, one's nature. A new name was always given when the candidate in the Mysteries was assumed to have put on the new nature of divinity. This is directly stated in *Revelation.*

Turning from Egyptian to Latin, we find this *na* introducing us to a new range of striking significance. In this language it is the base of one of the shortest verbs, whose stem is simply N- in the "A" conjugation, — that is. its accompanying vowel is "a" and not "e" or "i." This verb built up on the *na* stem. *nare*, means two things that at first do not suggest any kinship or connection. It means both "to be born" and "to swim." From it on the side of "born" we get *name, native, nature* and *natal;* on the side of "swim" we have *navy, naval, navel, natatorium* (a swimming pool), and probably our *natron* also. And how are being born and swimming connected? Any mother should know, or any physician: all birth is out of water, even that of all life on the earth out of the sea. "Moses" means drawn "out of the water." The Egyptian word for "birth" was *mes.* We find it in such Pharaonic names as Thothmes ("the born Thoth") and Rameses (the born god Ra) and others.

But more to the point, we have it in the word *Messiah*, the born Iah (Jah), the three letter name of Jehovah. The human babe comes forth *swimming* in a sack of water. That *Na* speaks very clearly to our intelligence indeed. Jesus said that the "*na*tural man" is born of *water*, while the "spiritual man" is born of air, as the Latin word "spiritus" means "air." How faithfully nature matches this spiritual history in her procedures! For the soul of life on our planet was born out of the water into the air, and the human foetus at birth steps out of water into the air!

This transition was by the ancient sages made the type-figure of the regeneration of man, when evolution brought him to the point of graduation from the reign of animal instinct, under the influence of natural as distinct from spiritual forces, over into the realm of mind (always symboled by air); and this becomes brilliantly illuminating if we keep before us the symbolic relation of the *na* of *na*tural to water, and that of spirit to air, in the Latin verb *spiro, I breathe.* And if we seek the absolutely first origin of this *na*'s connection with water, we have it, beyond all controversy of grammarians, back there in ancient Egypt's wondrous symbolic creations, in the hieroglyph that means water. In this archaic and arcane symbol-system, right in the Egyptian alphabet, the letter N is written in the form of *seven* wavelets of water, one might say it pictures the ocean agitated by the wind in seven waves, — /\/\/\/\/\/\ And the primary name attached to the divine ego-soul incarnated in matter-water-body was this letter thrice repeated, — NNN. Also the primitive name of the cosmic soul of being immersed in matter was *Nu.* This was the masculine form of the name, while the great universal mother-matter form of the name was *Nut,* and the form that indicated the universal undifferentiated essence of primal being at the start was the *Nun.*

When the Palestine religionists reformulated the body of their religious concepts, which they drew from ancient Egypt, they switched the alphabetical sign of water from N over to M, and just about all words signifying water-matter begin with M ever since. The reasons for this transfer the present writer has not discovered anywhere in his research. But there is no gainsaying the fact of it. Our own written English M still represents three of these original seven waves of water (printed form only two), and our written and printed N still represents two waves. While the Hebrew word for water in the sense of the sea is *iam*, the Hebrew word for water as such is *mayim*, which, being a plural (ending in *im*) would really be waters or waves.

And how vividly instructive this pursuit of meaning in the construction of words can become is well illustrated here when we consider the Hebrew word for "heaven." The first chapter of *Genesis* speaks of the general concept of heaven in the phrase translated "the waters of the firmament." But the firmament, that is, the underlying indestructible first essence of all creation, was always represented as dual, divided into the firmament above and the firmament below. The Egyptian savants had divided the creation into the Upper Nun and the Lower Nun. This would refer to the division of the primordial undifferentiated homogeneous matter — the NUN — into the masculine (spiritual) NU and the feminine (material) NUT, in life's universal polarity in the periods of manifestation, when it is not dormant in its phase of unmanifestation, called by the Hindus *pralaya*. This would give precisely what *Genesis* does give in its very first verse: "In the beginning God created the heavens (the Upper Nun) and the earth (the Lower Nun)." Now all things pertaining to the material or Lower Nun side of life's eternal duality, were symbolized by the two "lower" elements, earth and water; likewise all things pertaining to the Upper Nun side were symbolized by the two "higher" elements, air and fire. How clearly nature both sanctions and typifies this is seen in the fact that on the earth below we have earth and water, while above we have air and (the sun's) fire. Also we have fire in the upper air in the form of lightning, in a thunderstorm.

FIRE ON HEAVEN'S HEARTH

Water, however, is not confined solely to earth, but in the forms of vapor, visible as cloud, or rain, and invisible as rarefied water vapor, pervades the earth's upper regions. But here we have, in the Hebrew concept of the heavens, the idea of heaven as the place where the waters of the Upper Firmament are associated with fire, — sun or lightning. Hence to the word for water, *mayim*, they prefixed that great letter of their alphabet which is the symbol for *fire*, the letter *shin*, and this gives the word for "heaven" as *Sh'mayim*. This would convey all that range of meaning which flows from the idea of the original fiery power of the divine mind or spirit of God, interfusing itself in the essence of water-matter, to beget the universes. The waters of the Lower Firmament would be *mayim*, those of the Upper Firmament would be *sh'mayim*. How astonishingly these basic concepts find both illustration and corroboration in nature is seen when we reflect that the sound of this dynamic letter SH, meaning fire, is actually produced when one introduces fire into water; the hissing, sizzling sound. Actually in this naturograph we have in vivid pictorialization the basic idea involved in the creation itself, that is, the projection from God of the fiery power of his creative energies and their being injected into the innermost core or womb of matter. This is what is meant by the statements found in Hindu religious literature that the birth of creation took place or began with the shooting of the cosmic ray of *Purusha*, eternal Spirit, into the womb of *Prakriti*, or matter, the eternal universal Mother.

With an explosive bang that the human mind will never forget modern science has demonstrated the fact of staggering significance that all matter is, one might say, on fire with energy. And, trembling with a wondering anticipation of the next even more staggering discovery that will forever rock the human mind, and end forever the age-old controversy between materialism and idealism, over the question whether the primordial energy that created the universe is merely *physical force*, or the power of thinking mind, the intellect of man approaches closer and closer to the recognition that the ultimate and original force that generated life and being must be Mind. Science has now resolved matter back into pure force, into energy; matter is energy that has somehow cooled down, and like anything gaseous or fluid that cools down, it has "jelled," become static, grown hard. It has crystallized and settled into concrete state. And having demonstrated this stupendous fact, now the speculative prying mind of man awaits in trembling suspense the confirmation of the next world-shaking idea, that energy is itself the potency of Thinking Mind.

A phenomenon of modern life that has forced itself on our attention in the midst of the endless panorama of scientific discovery and achievement is the surprised recognition that much of the substance of our latest attainment in knowledge seems to have been in the possession of certain of the ancient peoples, more particularly the Egyptians, from whom it is evident that the sagacious Greeks derived the principia of the philosophical systematism which they developed to such grandiose heights in the Periclean period, some four centuries B.C. Hardly less brilliant was the rekindling of that light of the Platonic age which flared up after the dimming of the great flame following the fall of Athens, in the movement of what is known as Neoplatonism, about the second century A.D., when Ammonias Saccas established his school of "esoteric wisdom." This effort produced Numenius and Maximius of

Tyre, after whom came four giants of the philosophical world, Plotinus, Proclus, Porphyry and Iamblichus. Running like a thread of fire all through the master works of this group, — to which a little later Plutarch may be added — is the idea that the primary protyle, or first essence of which the creation is composed, the "stuff" of which all things are made, is, as modern thought suspects may be the very miracle of truth, — is in very fact Mind!

Yes, affirm these profound thinkers, not only is matter crystallized force, energy; that energy in turn is fluid Mind. Buried for these many centuries in the forgotten books of these great philosophers, to be specific, in the magnificent work entitled *The Six Books of Proclus on the Theology of Plato,* there has stood a sentence, which had it been brought out and kept in recognition, might well have saved Europe fifteen hundred years of its Dark Ages, and brought modern science that much sooner: *"The light of the sun is the pure energy of Intellect."* No one can fail to see the redoubtable challenge of this pronouncement out of the wisdom of the long past. It makes pertinent the question whether, with all the present incredible scientific marvels, we have yet caught up with the acumen of ancient Egypt and Greece. For there is evidence that those sapient Egyptian priests, as likewise the Chaldean "astrologers," had at least a theoretical knowledge of the nature and constitution of the atom, though, so far as we would judge, no cyclotrons to demonstrate the physical actuality. The profundity of Platonic and then the Neoplatonic philosophy is an undiminished marvel in universities, where they are still studied. If these, and perhaps even Hindu thinkers had knowledge that the fiery force of Mind flamed on the hearthstone of every atom, they were theoretically in advance of where we stand today. We have made the discovery that the thinking process in the human brain generates both heat and light, or electric energy. Experiments conducted by attaching to the heads of students a sensitive electrical device registered the generation of small quantities of force sufficient to light up a small electric bulb and run a tiny motor.

The Scriptures have analogized the mental creation of the universe in the Biblical phrase: "God spake, and the worlds sprang into existence." But back of all speech is thought. So it might be said that "what God hath wrought is what God hath first thought." If the evidence for this connection of creative energy with creative Mind is conclusive, we have a final — and welcome — settlement of the eternal squabble over the question of the nature and constituency of the universe; and the laurel wreath goes to idealism. The universe is the expression of the supreme divine Intellect, its majestic ideas having become concreted in what we have called matter. By an omnipresent instinct of reflecting intelligence, men have universally thought of one tangible thing in the realm of life as the appropriate symbol of all mental intelligence in the human area of consciousness, — the thing we call LIGHT. And we have found Proclus asserting that the light of suns is the pure radiance of Intellect. What a concept this gives us as we gaze into the "heavens" of a clear dark night, and see the infinite hosts of those suns twinkling through the dark of space! For if Proclus is right, those infinite points of light are the scintillating *brain cells* of the Mind of God! It is declared that a normal human brain has four quadrillion brain cells. We can generously allow God a few quintillions at least. We can see some billions, even if we can not count them. We have now proved that brain cells are very, very tiny — on our scale of relative proportions — units of the same energy that glows, seethes in flames of thousands of miles dimension on the surface of the sun, yet we know that in proportion to their size they are as far apart from each other as are the suns in the spread of space. Here is perfect analogy, and if the Scriptures do not speak utter nonsense when they declare that man is made in the image of God, they mean that our brain cells match his, and his match ours, in function and in kind.

Man is declared in the secret wisdom of the ancient sages to be the microcosm, but still a full duplicate of the macrocosm. And Hermes of Egypt, probably the sagest of earth's great sages. called by the Greeks "thrice-greatest," put this basic principle of understanding clearly before us in his ever-memorable statement: "True without falsehood, certain and most true, that which is above is as that which is below, and that which is below is as that which is above, for the performance of the miracle of the One Thing." And the Sophists of Athens said: "Man is the measure of all things." He has to be; for if he is the universe in miniature, he has to gauge all things by himself. Hence the Greeks adjured us: "Man, know thyself, and thou wilt know all things." Hence also the ancient seers warned men of the folly and the danger of worshipping any supposedly divine power outside their own being and nature. since all the power of the creation was already impounded in the confines of a human life. needing only development to bring it to "the fullness of the Godhood bodily."

Water below. and fire above. in the cosmos. in man. is the manifest order of things. As for man, the below is his body, composed seven-eighths of water; the above is the fiery energy of thinking mind in his quadrillions of brain cells. In the phrase of the poet, in the being of man "heaven and earth have kissed each other." More than that. under the stress of polarity. they have entered into a mutual relationship in which they are destined to woo. win and wed each other. and in generation after generation give birth in their wedlock to new stages of the creation.

In the mass of legendary fable concocted by the semantic genius of those sages of olden time was the tradition that when Messiah appeared, he would *come up out of the sea*. Truly enough now, with our eyes conditioned to a sort of new infra-red power to pierce the darkness in which the arcane cryptic figurism has been enshrouded, we can see how clearly this form of legendry tells the truth. For of course, since the "life of the soul," as the Scriptures tell us, "is in the blood," the divine power that will rise to deify us must come up out of the sea-water endowed with the electric potency that is found to reside in the ocean waters. It should be realized that the blood is electrically charged, is itself dynamic with a measure of the magic of the suns. Were it not so, the mere physical force of the heart's pumping could not drive it out through the fine channels of the veins and draw it all back again. All cells of the body share the life that animates the whole, and it is certain that the veinous and arterial channel walls furnish some pumping power, some constriction and expansion in rhythm to push the blood along, in aid of the heart.

If viewed from the purely mechanistic or purely materialistic standpoint man is just a machine. The mistake of materialist thought is in supposing that he is *just* a machine. He is a machine that is alive and is in every cell, to its degree, a thinking machine. We will approximate a truer view of man if we think of him as we might of a great printing press, every part of which, not dead but consciously alive, keeps feeling, thinking and voluntarily exerting itself to perform its function in the economy of the whole operation of printing. Had the world held on to this living conception of man, which it inherited from the occult legacy of a Golden Age in early human history, when, it is the legend, the gods still mingled with earth's inhabitants, a rosier cinematograph would have been the panorama of the last two thousand years of the world's dark record. The mechanistic, that is, the *dead* mechanistic concept of man's nature, has been the index of the world's, most particularly the Western world's, degradation of man's own concept of himself. As far as it can go, this concept takes no account of the inner spontaneous and unconquerable instincts and feelings welling up within the human consciousness, a hard cold posture of mind which tends to chill, to freeze and deaden the dynamic free-acting forces generically innate in the human constitution. The influence of the conscious mind upon the operation of the unconscious processes of the body, such as breathing, digestion, assimilation, heart beat, is not accurately known, but it must be unquestionably great. Therefore the thought that one's body is a machine of purely non-living parts, which work by purely physical, and not by biophysical laws and chemistries, is itself a force that will tend to slow and deaden the body's living activities. How potently a philosophy that pours into the body the power of a mental conception of its free-flowing, self-initiating mind energies would affect well-being for the human organism has been well attested by the more or less "miraculous" cures and healings registered by the upsurge of faith, confidence, hope and other positive attitudes of mind. Perhaps the most efficacious conception that the human individual can hold with regard to his own life and well-being is the idea that he is a dynamo of vibrant intelligent energy, a quantum of the conscious thinking Power that has generated and eternally activates the creation. If his thought lacks this element of the efficacy of spirit, he hardens his life and tightens around himself the prison walls that confine the free forces of his soul within the habitation they have built for their expression in the incarnation process. They are turned into a rigid, cumbersome incubus on the soul instead of being the plastic adaptive instrument for the soul's free expression. As Browning put it, "wall upon wall, the gross flesh hems it in." And another poet has spoken of the soul as "cribbed, cabined and confined" in the body. In fact this aspect of the soul's life received such emphasis in the great Greek philosophy that always the body was dramatized as not only the prison-house of the soul, but even its grave and tomb, since, when the soul descended into body, its subjection to the slow, sluggish tempo of the fleshly vehicle threw it into a torpor, a coma, a kind of actual "death," from which it had in the final outcome of its evolution to be resurrected. The Greeks in fact used practically the same word for "body" as for "tomb," the former being *soma* and the latter *sema*.

One can see the aptness of this symbolism when resort is again had to the typology of water for the body element and fire for the soul force. For naturally water extinguishes fire, kills it. St. Paul (*Romans* 7) says that the incarnation of his soul in body killed him. But, he added, he will regain his life. have his resurrection, through the power of the Lord Jesus Christ, which will overcome "the body of this death" and grant him life eternal. The ancient wise men, those Egyptian priests, always thought of soul entering body for its life work under the figure of fire plunging into water, or soul crossing the "Red Sea," meaning by this sea the body's blood. Such conceptions and figures held thought in fluidity and tended to keep the body plastic, so as to be responsive to the impact of the thought power of the central brain intelligence upon the nerve life of all the cells of the body. Whatever possibility man has of living a radiant life inhered in this sort of mental attitude, which a materialist philosophy chills to inanity.

One will find a strange fact of momentous significance in this connection right in the dictionary. It is that the great body of verbs indicating the initiation of movement begin with the letter "s" or its equivalent "sh." These are the letters which start, shove off all kinds of movement, such as strike, slap, stamp, smite, speak, slide, streak, skate, send, shoot, spear, slip, slump, spit, stride, step, sneak, steal, scrape, scream, sing and scores more. That this is no happy fancy of ours is confirmed by the definite fact that the ancient Egyptian language prefixed "s" (or "sh") to words denoting a state or condition, to make them mean the act of producing that state or condition. One example is *maat*, truth, from the stem *ma*, true, which when "s" is prefixed, becomes *sma*, meaning to confirm, establish, i.e., to "make true." This must have come from the fact that the introduction of soul into body (water) in incarnation, producing the "s" ("sh") sound, *started* all things off, set all things going for the life of the soul. That is, the letter's sound suggested the initial step in life. The extent to which the ancient sagacity resorted to poetic tropism of this kind would not be believed generally.

TURNING WATER INTO BLOOD.

All this analysis may have seemed to take the theme far from its base in the Red Sea. But as this symbol represents the human body, or its blood, and this constitutes the very basis of human life, and the body is inseparably linked with the soul, the Red Sea may be said to be the chief ingredient in all human problems, whether physical, religious, philosophical or psychological. If the human body is not an essential element in all man's problems, it would be so only under the conditions that Hindu religion seems so strongly to suggest to us mortals, that we may so spiritualize our consciousness that we may release the soul completely from the incubus of the flesh. We need to be reminded here of St. Paul's pointed assertion of the connection our souls sustain to the body, when he says: "For God, who has caused the light to shine out of the darkness hath shined in our hearts,...but *we have this treasure in earthen vessels*." This can be taken also in close connection with the statement of Greek philosophy: "I am a child of earth and the starry skies, but my race is of heaven alone." Yes, heaven is our true, original and basic home; but the Father sends us forth periodically from "that imperial palace whence we came," since it is the function of spirit or soul to impregnate matter with the dynamic of the divine Mind, so that all life, all the universe may reflect the thought of the creative brain.

The Judeo-Christian Scriptures — the "Bible" — do not contain material elaborating the semantic potential of the Red Sea symbolism comparable to what we find in the Egyptian, and doubtless other, literature. Yet there are touches which are decidedly significant, which, when taken in connection with those found especially in the great *Book of the Dead*, go far to corroborate the thesis herein developed. The most direct and surely a most cogent affirmation that the human body blood is sea water, in fact a most astonishing confirmation of it, is found in *Revelation* 8:8. Here indeed is a positive statement to the effect that the divine fire of soul went down into the sea "which is on the border of the earth" and did two things to it that should have meant far more to our slumbering cognitive faculties than they have appeared to do. First, it set the sea on fire; and, second, it turned the sea into blood.

Perhaps one of the most direct allegorical references to the expulsion of the Sons of God from heaven and their incarnation on earth is found in the eighth chapter, fifth verse of *Revelation*: "And the angel took the censer and filled it with fire of the altar and cast it into the earth." This was the sending of fire from the empyrean (*pyr* means "fire" in Greek) down to earth in the form of the hosts of angelic beings that were born of the mind of God, thus "immaculately conceived," that is, generated purely by spirit or mind energy unmixed, "uncontaminated" with

-32-

gross matter. This is matched in the Old Testament by the first emanation of the Ab-ra(m) power, the First Light out of Ur, the "city" of the Chasadim, and his going "west then south" into earthly incarnation, or "Egypt." Both Ra and Ur mean "fire," the first an Egyptian spelling and the second Babylonian. "Ur" is the original Chaldean word for "fire," becoming *pur (pyr)* later in Egypt. (Pur is the Greek word for "fire" still.) These heaven-conceived, mind-born Sons of God were called in Hindu systems the Agniswatha Pitris, fathers of the fire emanations, as *agni* is "fire" in Sanscrit. They have become immemmorially poetized as the "Divine Flames," "the Divine Sparks." Man's soul is a spark or ray of the divine creative Fire of Mind, as all profound religion declares.

"I come from the Sea of Flame," exclaims the soul in the Egyptian *Book of the Dead*, "from the Lake of Flame and the Sea of Fire; and I live." Speaking in the Egyptian drama the soul declares: "I am the Great One, son of the Great One; I am Fire, son of Fire, to whom was given his head after it was cut off." (The symbolism here represents the idea that, even as Plato depicted it, the soul, as it were, loses its head, its higher dimension of consciousness, when it decends into incarnation, and has to recover it by evolution here — Paradise lost, Paradise regained.)

We have all the legends of fire flaming forth out of the mouth, or the nostrils of God, consuming his enemies. This is often poetized as the "wrath of God" devastating all things. In *Deuteronomy* (32) we find the Deity telling of the awful power of his mind energy: "My wrath has flared up, flaming to the nether world itself, burning up the earth and all it bears, setting the roots of the hills ablaze." And again: "From Sinai came the Eternal....blazing in fire from the south." We remember how his presence on Mount Sinai was accompanied by lightning, smoke and flame. The seven golden candles of *Revelation* typify the seven rays of the divine emanation as it poured forth to create a seven-branched tree of life. The old English ritual of burning the Yule log on the hearth was to symbolize the lighting up and final transfiguration of the natural body and nature of man by the transforming power of the divine flame of spirit. The ropes binding Samson's arms, when "the spirit of the Eternal inspired him nightily, became like wax that has caught fire, the bonds melted off his hands." The Egyptians called the watery body of man "the Pool of the Double Fire," the dark, murky, smoky, smudgy fires of low sensualities; and the pure, clear, beautiful flame of compassion and love. The lower flares of the animal passions, it need hardly be pointed out, were the fires of hell. Happily no one need fear the prospect of being tortured in the fires of a post-mortem Hades, as we are living in all the "hell" we will ever experience right here on earth. That fire in our blood is all the hell we will ever have to dread. But we had better dread it now. All we need to do is to transmute those fires that burn in the blood with smudge, soot and smoke into the pure flames of a beauteous life. "For wickedness burneth as a fire. It shall devour the briars and thorns, and shall kindle in the thickets of the forests." These are the coarse underbrush of the hatreds, greeds and evil motives of our lives. If reason and discipline will not burn them out, pain eventually will.

Says the Greek philosopher Heraclitus: "Man is a portion of cosmic Fire, imprisoned in a body of earth and water." John the Baptist said that whereas he will give us the lower baptism of (earth and) water, the Christ coming after him will baptize us "with the Holy Air (*spiritus*, Latin, means "air.") and with fire." Jesus said: "I come to scatter fire upon the earth;" also "I beheld Satan like lightning fall from heaven." All these are references to the angelic hosts, God's own Sons, whom the Father dispatched to earth to do his work with his earthly children. "He hath made his angels messengers and his ministers a flame of fire.'' Spirit was universally symbolized by the element of fire, as was mind by air, emotion by water and sensation by earth. Our souls are sparks of the divine Flame.

The fiery nature of spirit is indicated in the symbolism by the figure of incense and the censer, the latter being the miniature ''stove'' in which the heavenly fire burned and gave off its pleasing incense for God's delectation. The censer, as a vessel which could contain and transport the fire of soul to earth, must refer to what St. Paul calls our ''spiritual body.'' Within man's outer physical body all religions of the arcane wisdom asserted that he has several finer bodies of sublimated essence, still in a sense material, but not of the gross physical matter familiar to our senses. Science now knows of the existence of matter in many ethereal-spiritual forms, impalpable and invisible, yet quite literally real; and these inner bodies hold or convey the central nucleus of soul when the outer physical body is thrown off, or not yet assumed. The intimation of the text of *Revelation*, then is that the ''angel,'' the power of God, having packed the soul in a finer spiritual body, whisks it off the altar and transports it down to earth.

Then two verses later on in that eighth chapter of *Revelation* the text says that the seven angels (creative life energy is always projected forth from the hearth (altar) of God's fire in seven impulsions) ''prepared themselves to sound.'' ''And the first angel sounded, and there followed hail and fire mingled with *blood*, and they were cast upon the earth.'' Here is the first mention of the divine fire's connection with blood. But once these sparks, or units, of the fiery mind essence were ensconced in the bodies of animal creatures here on earth, they became in a very real sense the fiery power of the body blood, the generators of the electric dynamism found in the blood. "For in the blood is the life of the soul," says the Scripture. Drain out a person's blood and the spark and fire, the dynamo of his life, is gone. The fire has gone out on his hearth.

But then in the next (eighth) verse comes the crowning statement of the truth we are enunciating: "And the second angel sounded, and as it were a great mountain burning with fire was cast into the sea; and the third part of the *sea became blood*."

The second century Christian protagonist, Justin Martyr, says that at the baptism of Jesus by John, "a fire was kindled in the waters of the Jordan." The actuality of the meaning hinted at by such poetic figures can be caught in quite realistic form when one says of some outrage that "it makes one's blood boil with indignation." Through the avenue of beautiful conceptual imagery we can come to a realization of what ancient poets meant when they speak of a fire blazing within the sea, and, as fire always does to water, converting it into steam or vapor and so enabling it to rise in the air.

The tenth verse rounds out this phase of the incarnation symbolism by saying: "And the third angel sounded, and there fell a great star from heaven, burning as it were a lamp, and it fell upon the third part of the rivers and upon the foundations of water."

The fifth angel's blast also brought a falling star to earth. This is the lightning streak of Satan falling to earth which Jesus says he beheld.

So the divine fire of soul migrating to earth, says the great allegory in *Revelation*, set the sea on fire, made it glow all *red* and turned it into blood. Will the Fundamental literalist, who insists that every word of the Scriptures is to be taken in its bald physical sense, protest to us that the Pacific Ocean is blood? A thing of this sort is quite happily available to reduce the claims of literalism to their proper category of ribald nonsense. But because such a construction of poetic fancy collapses into preposterous fol-de-rol when its literal actuality is insisted upon, let no one think that it therefore is to be discarded and put out of court as irrelevant and valueless. Its dynamic value only emerges when its claimed actual factuality is dropped and a truth structure is revealed to discerning vision deep within the frame of the outer allegory. Such was the form and method by which the ancient wise men depicted truth by symbol and allegory. Hence, truly enough, not in the seven seas of our globe, but on the very hearth of the life of mortal men, the heavenly fire conveyed to earth by God's own Sons, does dip down into the sea which is the watery essence of these mortal bodies of ours, and does set them aflame with a fire of life and soul and does turn them into blood. Who has not read over and over those mystifying verses of *Revelation's* flaring allegorism and wondered what those words really meant? Here at any rate is one luminous key that can turn on the light of intelligible, rational meaning.

But it is when we turn to old Egypt's prodigious tomes of hoary wisdom that we see the symbolism more openly and clearly at work. In commenting on Chapter 176 of the *Book of the Dead,* Budge, the noted Egyptologist, writes: "As fire and boiling water existed in the underworld (our earth) he (the soul) hastened to protect himself from burns and scalds by reciting these chapters." For the titles of these several chapters are: "Of drinking water and not being burned by fire in the underworld," and "Of not being scalded with water." Showing how closely Old Testament material must have related to its antecedent Egyptian sources, we find this symbolism very closely matched in *Isaiah* 43: "When thou passest through the waters I shall be with thee; and through the rivers, they shall not overflow thee; when thou walkest through the fire, thou shalt not be burned; neither shall the flame kindle on thee."

The imagery here, drawn straight from nature, from chemistry and physics, tells us in effect that when the celestial fire of God's mighty spirit is, by incarnation, introduced into the natural watery elements of the body, this fire is going to heat up this water, cause it to boil and seethe, so that we see a man in passion burning with hot zeal over some injury or affront. A burning within the sea, sure enough; the ocean on fire; the bush all aflame, yet was not consumed. If the soul, the god himself, who himself contributed the fire that heated the body blood, was not sufficiently in control, he stood a fair chance of being "scalded" by his own fiery rage. So the allegories represent the god-soul as being able to allay the storms on this sea of life, and fittingly enough, represent the tempests as raging when he, the power within the ship, lies fast asleep down in the "hold." So the Manes, or "shade" of the person in this underworld, prays in the Egyptian Ritual that he "may have power over the water and not be drowned." Emerging from his dangerous journey across the sea in victory, he chants: "I am the being who is never overwhelmed in the waters." Sargon of Assyria, who was picked up out of a wicker basket floating in the reeds (the "Reed Sea") by the river's brink by the king's daughter long before the same legend was repeated with Moses, exclaims: "My mother gave me to the river, which drowned me not." "Moses" means "drawn out of the water."

The Scriptures were found to give authoritative support to the symbolism of the sea being turned into blood, but it seemed unlikely that they would be found stating directly that this change came about as a result of the transfer of the stream of the earth's biological evolution of life forms from the oceans to the land. Yet even a direct statement of that effect was encountered in the course of recent searching for the data supporting the theses of this essay. Modern biological science and ancient fanciful semanticism find themselves in amazing accord in some verses in the early chapters of the book of *Exodus*. The fact of the change coming from the shifting of the evolution chain from sea to land finds absolutely astonishing literal confirmation in *Exodus* 4:9. The ancient allegorist — or perhaps it was the translator — substitutes the word ''river'' for ''sea,'' but that in no way alters the sense. It is still the earth's great water-body that is referred to. Speaking to Moses for the children of Israel, the Lord directs him to ''take of the water of the river and pour it upon the dry land: and the water which thou takest out of the river *shall become blood upon the dry land.*'' The idea is hinted at again in *Exodus* 7:17, the Lord speaking: ''I will smite with the rod that is in mine hand upon the waters which are in the river, and they *shall be turned to blood.*'' Again in verse 19 the Lord commands Aaron to stretch out his rod and his hand over the waters of ''Egypt'' ''that they may be blood throughout all the land of Egypt.'' (Most high-ranking scholars regard this ''Egypt'' of the *Exodus* narrative as a glyph for the earth and the human body, being the nadir point to which souls descend for incarnation, and also as the fabled ''underworld'' of mythology.) As it is obvious that the Pacific Ocean has *not* turned to blood anywhere else than in the human bodies of earth's people, one must realize that the piercing vision of the seer of old had hidden a salient truth of biological evolution beneath the allegory. If our Bible is found to be talking about *this* kind of truth we had better read it a bit more closely and with an eye alert to pierce semantic veils for the discovery of more cryptic reference.

Then there is (in verse 21) the statement that the catalytic power of the "rod" of spiritual fire so changed the water of the river that the Egyptians could no longer drink of it, because it "stank," which is obvious enough reference to its unpotable brackish taste. So then "the Egyptians digged round about the river for water to drink." If a spiritual interpretation of this last symbolism is sought, it may perhaps be found in the idea that, as the sea water stands for the basic natural life of man, this life of sense, animalism and lower appetencies will in the course of time and evolution become repugnant to the soul and it seeks refreshment from the purer aspirations of the spirit.

Could anything in the sacred writings be more significant and illuminating than the announcement that man undergoes two baptisms, and as it were, two births, first that of water, then that of fire? (Ancient insight always assigned *two mothers* to the Christ figures.) As water not only typifies, but virtually *is* the body, the first baptism depicts the experience the soul undergoes when its divine fire of spirit is submerged in the waters of the Lower Nun, that is, incarnated in earthly watery body. This phase of the incarnational ordeal involves all the forms of experience that can accrue to man through the intermixture of the two sides or segments of his dual being, his body and his soul, and could only be symbolized adequately by all the phenomena that are generated when fire meets and combats water. For a long time the "watery" elements of consciousness, sense and emotion (earth and water), predominate and rule the individual's life. But gradually, and all too slowly, the pure and more powerful flames of reason and love gain the ascendency. Inevitably in the end the more powerful element must win out, and this at once introduces the great symbolism of fire drying up the water. And here we have the ground of all those allegories of the God-power drying up the waters of a sea or river in order that the Sons of God (in the Old Testament the Israelites — who incidentally are *not* the Hebrews as a nation or race, but purely a spiritual grouping) may cross over without being drowned. When the "sea" starts to burn, it will in the end be dried up. And with this comes one of the most startling revelations of esoteric significance in all the realm of symbolic depiction of truth: the truth as to the conversion of sinful man into man sinless and divine. For as the "sinning" nature of the first and unredeemed Adam is symbolized by water, and water by nature falls, the action upon it by the application to it of the fiery power of the divine soul, which will vaporize it, converts it into a state analogous to steam, a form in which it, too, like fire, shall rise again. What moral lesson could be more cogent than the realization that if man lives in the realm of base passion, he will continue to fall; but that if he will purge his carnal sensualities of their gross selfish character, he will arise! So St. Paul descants endlessly on the theme that the indulgence of the interests of the flesh means death, whereas the cultivation of the interests of the spirit means life and peace. To descend into and remain bound under the "watery" nature of the body and its sensual instincts is, in the great theology of the Greeks, a virtual death; to "dry out" these heavy, sluggish motivations by the superior power of the rational soul is to achieve the resurrection.

The Scriptures speak figuratively of the power of God as "rebuking" the sea and "smiting the sea," confounding the sea. This depicts the spirit's power to check, change and ultimately destroy the force of the lower motivations of the "flesh," the Old Man of the Sea." Doubtless this is the origin of the poetic phrase, "to suffer a sea change." Translated into terms of modern psychology, this typism would have relevance to the function of the superconscious power of the great "unconscious" in man to check, control and redirect the energies of the conscious part of his psychism. When the interpreters of the Scriptures can show that the meaning so cryptically disguised under glyph and symbol has immediate pertinence to the psyche and the spiritual life of all mortals, the great legacy of ancient Holy Writ will be able to reassert its benignant influence

ICHTHYS, THE GREAT FISH

As all parts and elements of the natural world were instinct with symbolic intimations for the discerning mind of ancient semanticists, that which the sea so voluminously generates, its living product, the fish, could not escape the search for meaningful signification. How prolifically we have the great symbol utilized in the archaic representations! Mythology teems with the recurrence of the whales, the dolphins that transport the heroes across the waters, the sea-serpents that attempt to strangle infant deities, monsters of the deep and plain common fish that serve as food, or one that turns up with a gold coin in its mouth. The intimations of symbolic meaning of the fish typograph are among the profoundest in the realm of ancient semanticism. A few of these must be examined.

Striking indeed is it that we find the fish to be the monographic symbol of the Christ himself in the initial stages of the inception of Christianity. There was much reason for the Church leaders, such as Augustine and Tertullian, to speak of Jesus as the Great Fish in the sea, and his followers, the Christians, as the little minnows. For in Greek emblemism the Christ figure was typified as the great fish, Pisces of the zodiac. This was inevitable when one knows of the addiction of the inspired religious mind of the ancient day to the custom of making the zodiac serve as the graph of all esoteric significance. This is itself a vast, complex and deeply recondite study, seemingly fathomless in the profundity and cogency of its implications for understanding the religious life of man.

Most simply defined, the zodiac is a figure depicting the journey of the sun through the cycle of the twelve sections of the heavens, both in the period of its earthly annual revolution, or in that of the full cycle of the precession of the equinoxes through the whole twelve houses of the sky in 25,868 years, known as the Great Cycle. The smaller annual cycle was a miniature of the great precessional cycle and served equally well for typology. In the spirit of this symbology it was the custom of the ancient sages of the divine wisdom to typify and designate the power of the coming Christos under the name and nature of the sign of the zodiac in which the sun stood for approximately 2160 years of its stasis in each house. For instance, in the sign of Leo the Christ power was, in the region dominated by Jewish religionism, the Lion of Judah. Under the Cancer sign the Egyptians dubbed it the sacred Scarab, Cancer having been the sign of the beetle before it was that of the Crab. With the sun in Gemini, the divine nature was the dual force of good and evil, the twin brothers, symboled by the stars Castor and Pollux in the sky. In Taurus, the Egyptians, Chaldeans and even the Israelites worshipped the divine power under the symbol of the sacred Bull, the Golden Calf, the Cow of Isis and other goddesses, In Aries, the Ram, the great symbol of the Son of God was of course the sacrificial Lamb, and in Greek mythology the Golden Fleece. And when Christianity was taking form, the sun was making the transit from Aries into Pisces, the sign of the two Fishes. Hence the Ram and Lamb symbolism still prevailed, but the Piscean figurism was being introduced, and its presence in the Christian literature and even in the religion's early iconography is surprisingly in evidence.

The astute-minded Greeks, dealing with the Christos concept in this intriguing fashion, therefore portrayed the divine Avatar for the Piscean era as the Great Fish, and a myth like the Jonah-whale fabrication was inevitable. The ancient Sumerians, ancestors of the Babylonians, had spoken of the Fish incarnation of Vishnu, and the ancient eponymous hero of the Chaldeans was Ioannes, the Fish Avatar, under the name of Dagon. And *dag* is the Hebrew word for "fish."

But the Greeks ingeniously took their word for "fish," which is Ichthys (Ichthus) and, using each letter of the again over the lives of all men.

word as the initial of a word, coined the sentence-phrase: IESOUS CHRISTOS, THEOU UIOS SOTER; which reads: Jesus Christ, Son of God, Savior. It is known as the Ichthys monograph of Christ, the "Fish Avatar" of the Greeks.

Such was the general vogue of this fish-image of divinity that, using a Latinized form of the word, the Greeks in the early years of the Christian movement, habitually referred to the Christians as the *Pisciculi* (Latin: *piscis*, "fish"), meaning the "little fishes." It was just a popular exploitation of the figurative flourish of the zodiacal symbol, with a touch perhaps of slight derision. It could be that the appellation was flavored with a bit of scurrility or mild contempt, as the Christians were universally regarded, in the inception of their fanatical upsurge of ignorant pietism, as pitiably deluded religious zealots. In fact the very name — Christians — was first fastened on them at Antioch, the book of *Acts* states, as a term properly ridiculing people who were so unintelligent as to believe that the Christos, yes, even the Logos, the unthinkable power that created the galaxies of the cosmos, was walking around down here on earth ensconced in the body of a man said to have been a carpenter in Galilee. They claimed that this obscure and obviously deluded countryside preacher and prophesier of the swift coming of the Kingdom of God, in which he was to sit in glory perpetual on the right hand of the Eternal God, was the "Fish Avatar" of the Absolute Deity. To philosophical Greeks this idea that the infinite power predicated in their great concepts represented by the words "Christos" and "Logos," the Second Person of the cosmic Trinity, could be compressed in the body of a man of our human order was incredibly crude, naive and preposterous; and the cultured Greeks, as also the Romans, held them in supreme contempt as pitiably ignorant pietists, as we think of certain sects in our civilization today who continue to predict the immediate coming of the Christ, and the "end of the world."

But perhaps the most telltale evidence of the astrological symbolism connected with Christianity is the pointedly significant fact that the Galilean Messiah's twelve disciples were declared to be "fishermen." Christian theological lucubration has never once had the candor to face the devastating challenge which this obvious link with zodiacal symbolism presents to the claimed historicity of the Gospels. If there were in historical actuality twelve men attached to the Judean claimant for the mantle of Messiahship, they would have "inherited" the designation of "fishermen," no matter if they were farmers, herdsmen, tradesmen, or as Matthew was, a tax collector, a publican, simply by virtue of the semantic spirit of the religious traditions of the age, for the Sabaean constructions of Chaldean astrology, projected in occult circles almost as a pictorial Bible, were universally rife among the Mystery groups, the Gnostics, Manichaeans, Essenes and other associations of mystical-occult bent. Under Aries symbolism they would have been "shepherds," and under Taurian, "cowherds," under Capricorn "goatherdsmen."

Then the Christians themselves adopted the two fishes of the Piscean sign as their own emblem. In the catacombs of Rome the dual fish monogram was everywhere in evidence, carved or pictured in many ways, even on the forehead of the images of the Christ, and on the walls and altars. And Jesus instructed Peter to find the gold coin wherewith to pay the tax levy in the fish's mouth; and he said: "I will make you fishers of men;" and his last wonderwork was the miraculous draught of fishes that broke the net. The fish's bladder, in Latin the *Vesica Piscis*, was utilized as a symbol of the presence of air in the water, intimating the presence of mind (air) in the body (water). Fish also was a symbol of divine food for man, since his soul, once it was immersed in the "sea" in incarnation, would find fish his most natural food. The great religious Ritual of Egypt (*Book of the Dead*) dramatizes the god as declaring: "I am the great and mighty Fish which was in the city of Qem-Ur." And a statement is that he shall in the end be freed from the great Abtu fish, meaning that he, like Jonah released from the whale after three days, would be liberated from the necessity of further incarnation. Likewise the Egyptians pictured the goddess Neith (whose name Gerald Massey equates with "net") as fishing Horus, the Christ, out of the sea, as the Pharaoh's daughter fishes Moses out of the waters among the *reeds*. At least two of the prominent goddesses of the Eastern Mediterranean region, Atergatis and Semiramis, were called "Fish Mothers." And on the head of Neith, an earlier form of the goddess Hathor, there was inscribed a perch. Neith carried the shuttle or knitter, for the weaving of her fish-nets.

The emblem of the goddess catching the Son of God as a fish in her net would dramatize the simple fact of incarnation, to begin with, as the feminine is matter (its symbol is water) and matter catches the incarnating souls in its meshes. But as the ordeal of life in the sea of matter eventually lifts the captured souls out of this realm of incarnate life into the world of spirit (air), even so also the act of fishing emblemed the release of souls from their captivity in the body, the "Red Sea." The fish floating about in the water is the most forceful symbol of organic life immersed in inorganic matter, and that is precisely what the fish symbol most cogently portrayed. A fish in the sea almost shouts at us the fact of our being divine souls, the product of organic evolution, immersed and floating about in the sea of inorganic atomic matter. A phrase from an archaic formulary, expressing concisely the basic idea of souls incarnated in matter, referred to them as "suffering under the *dense sea*" of matter. Perhaps the future stability of the edifice of the Christian religion may be severly shaken from the startling revelation that the Greek word for "sea" is pontos, and for "dense" is piletos, which would take the form in Latin of "Pontius Pilate." We can only ask: can this etymology be the origin of the creed's phrase: "He suffered under Pontius Pilate?"

But another line of research leads us to further amazing disclosures in this "fishing expedition." It has been shown earlier that the ancient original Egyptian short name of the primordial undifferentiated sea of being, so to say our "empty space," was NU; its masculine (spiritual) manifestation was NUN; and its feminine (material) polar opposite, was NUT. It has just been said that the primary symbolism of the fish floating in the sea was the image of units of divine spirit-souls (always masculine) immersed in the water of incarnation. The term NUN, then, would by sheer emblemism represent spirit in matter, and at man's level and station in evolution, the soul in the body. The cosmic NUN being the great Father spirit, we surprisingly find that in Chaldean and Syriac NUN means the Great Fish, symbolized in the heavens as the constellation of Cetus the Whale! The Sons of God, his little "fish" children, would be the offspring of this Great Fish, or Sons of NUN. Following this guiding thread we run into such an amazing correlation of ideas and symbols as fairly to stagger our minds with the marvel of it all.

First of all, and almost an immediate knockout for us, we find that all ancient astrological formulations represented the Christ characters as being born in the house or sign of Pisces; all were sons of the "Fish Mothers." This was inevitable from the fact of semantic science that the first or natural man in our dual nature, being the son of the Virgin, had to be represented as being born in Virgo. But the spiritual man, his direct polar opposite would then have to be born exactly across the zodiac from Virgo, and that brought the second or spiritual birth in Pisces, six months later. And in the first chapter of *Luke's* Gospel Jesus, the Christ, is declared to have been born just six months after his natural-man forerunner, John the Baptist! In all Christian typology, Jesus was fairly swamped with the fish symbolism, as has been shown above.

What, then, on top of that, is our astonishment when we find that there was another Jesus away back there in the Old Testament; yes, a man with the Jesus name, one of the dozen or more variant spellings of this name Jesus, but still Jesus, — namely Joshua! And whose son was he? Joshua, son of N U N! Here was Jesus by name, and this time connected with descent from the fatherhood represented by the Great Fish!

Still further heightening the wonder comes the next datum: in the Hebrew alphabet every letter has a corollary designation, a "nick-name" so to say, which gives some recondite intimation of its function in the canon of sounds and signs which make up the alphabet. *Aleph* (A) means, for instance, *ox; beth* (B) means *house; gimel* (G) means *camel; daleth* (D) means *door*, etc. When we come to the middle of the alphabet, which point represents the lowest level of matter into which the fire of soul descends before it turns to return back to the heaven of spirit, and is therefore the place of water, matter's eternal symbol, we find that M is the Hebrew hieroglyph for waves of water, as N is in Egyptian, and its alphabetical name is *mem* and means *water*l and that N — brace yourselves for a jolt — has for its nick-name *fish* and, of all things wonderful, is called NUN. M is *mem*; N is *nun*. It is well to see what we have together here: Joshua (Jesus) born in Pisces, even in Christianity, and son of Nun, the Fish! Jesus, Son of Nun!

Virgo was called the "house of bread," that divine Bread that Jesus said came down from heaven and was made man, as Christ, the God in man. Pisces was the house of the Great Fish, or the dual fishes. Bread and fish were therefore made the symbolic dual food for man, the one physical and the other spiritual nourishment. Most wonderfully in old Egypt's semantic science, the cities were often named from some function of the deific life. A city in which it was symbolically said that Horus, the Christ, was born and died, was *Anu*, which becomes *Any* when transferred to English (the Greek "u" always turning to English "y".) A very significant item mentions it as "the place of *multiplying* the divine bread." The birth of the Christ soul in all men surely multiplies that heavenly Bread, broken for all souls at the Eucharist. So, through association with Virgo and its symbolic name, the house of bread, the opposite house of Pisces, house of the fish, merged its emblemism with its polar opposite, and the two symbols, bread and fish, became the twin forms of man's divine food. Should we be, then, too stunningly struck with amazement when we find that our New Testament Gospels themselves contain the allegory of the Christ character feeding a *multitide* of people, enhungered *after three days*, by miraculously *multiplying* bread and its companion symbol, fish? And where did this multiplication of the divine food take place in the Gospels? Yes, at this same town, Any (Anu), to which the Hebrews had at some date prefixed their word for "house" *(beth)* simply to give its astrological reference as the zodiacal "house of bread," and thus it became — Beth-Any, Bethany! So both in ancient Egypt and in the Hebrew-Christian Scriptures the Christ figure dramatized the miracle of feeding the multitude of mortals in this symbolic city of Anu by multiplying the divine bread and fish.

Are we ready, then, for the next flash of realization of great discovery which darts out from the philological intimations of this name, the "house of bread?" It flashes upon us when we simply ask how one says "house of bread" in Hebrew, ordinary Hebrew. For the answer to that is none other than the astonishing word — *Beth* (house), *lehem* (bread) — Bethlehem! Bethlehem is Bethany, house of combined bread and fish. For the Christ, as Jesus says positively, is the product of two births, the one natural, of *water*; the other spiritual, of spirit *(fire)*; or of bread (Virgo) and fish (Pisces). "Ye must be born again," he said; born of water and the spirit-fire. Virgo is the first great Mother of life, formless inchoate matter, the *Virgin* Motherhood; and her name was almost everywhere a form of the name for *sea* or *water*. Pisces in the zodiac represented the *second* Mother of life, organic matter that has been impregnated by the rays of the divine sun of life, or divine spirit. Virgo can give birth only to natural man; Pisces gives birth to the spirit-soul, which matter inorganic could not do. Pisces *is* the Fish, the symbol of organic life born out of the *sea*, so that its Christly offspring, the Christs themselves, are all fished up out of the sea. (Recall that a legend said that the Messiah was to come up out of the *sea*.)

In one facet of ancient symbolism all life was said to have emanated from the Fish's mouth. In the uranograph, or chart of the heavens, the stream of life was pictured as flowing forth from the constellation in the southern sky called the Southern Fish, to correspond to that of Cetus, the Whale, in the northern sky. Thence it flowed north and emptied its stream just under the foot of the constellation of Orion. This great cluster of bright stars seen in our sky of winter was, in ancient astrological portrayal, the representative of the Christ. Orion was the mighty hunter, followed by his dog — the great Dog Star Sirius — by which was meant that the power of the divine mind, seeking to stamp the shape of its creative ideas upon all matter, led the way of evolution, while behind it trailed the animal, the faithful dog, the body! Mythology had it that Orion was pressing on in pursuit of the Pleiades, that cluster of six stars some little distance ahead of him, called the Seven Sisters, but with one star missing. The subtle intimations here can be only that spirit must seek to express itself through the agency of the natural world, nature being feminine always, and also eternally structuralized upon the basis of the creational number *seven*. That one is as yet missing is likely to intimate that, since all the cycles of evolving life manifest six formations of physical substance, or planes of existence for the expression of their creative forces, the spiritual mind-power which this structuralization of cosmic energy is destined to express, not being physical, but spiritual, is not manifest in visible form with its six-fold basis. Let us remember that creation covers *six* days, and not seven, God resting on that cosmic Sabbath from his labors. The physical universe is always the visible side; the cosmic mind power that each cycle demonstrates by the work it produces at six levels, is invisible.

If imagery of this sort seems overly subtle and a bit thin in spots, it must be realized that the religious mind of the ancient day disported itself, so to say, in sallies of fancy of this kind; and if one will follow them closely, they will be found to adumbrate the soundest and unassailable truth. And the truths thus intimated are always deeply related to man's inner life and experience, are in fact the deepest truths that the human mind can grasp.

Well, then, if the fish is the symbol of organic life generated out of the inorganic, the ancient starry drama would represent that the stream of organic life emenates from the substrate matter of the physical universe, from the very womb of matter, as the sages like to phrase it often, when evolution has developed it to its supreme organic unity of function, and thence it proceeds up the path of growth and development until it reaches the state of godhood symbolized by Orion. In brief it says that the stream of organic evolution, arising out of the sea, reaches its high goal of godhood in Orion. It is to be noted that the astrological depiction does not give it as arising out of the water directly, but out of the Southern *Fish*, itself the product of a long evolution of organic structure arising out of the inorganic virgin matter. It is important to clarify this double-stage procedure of the drama of creation, for inorganic matter could not generate self-conscious mind in creatures starting at the bottom of the scale of manifest being. Inorganic matter was the "Old First Mother," and could give birth only to organic matter, considered as her daughter. The daughter, then, in turn, since she through the instrumentality of her highly developed specialized functionism such as brain and nerves *could* give birth to mind, reason, will and love in her creatures, would thus be the second mother and her child the Christ. In zodiacal terms the Virgo — Mother energy of matter, could not herself birth the Christ, but could produce her own daughter, Pisces, who representing the organic universe, *could* bear the Christ consciousness in the brains and hearts of her offspring. Virgo had first to bear Pisces, and Pisces in turn bore the Christ. All ancient Sun-Gods and Saviors were "born" in the house of Pisces, the house of (fish and) bread, Bethlehem.

This item has been elaborated at length for the reason that, though few realize it, it is all found in the Gospel narrative in the New Testament. All the ancient Christs were said to have two mothers, the First Old Mother, and the Second or spiritual Mother. In the Egyptian system they were the goddess sisters and twins, Isis and Nephthys.

The myth said that Isis conceived the divine Son Horus and Nephthys gave him birth. Changing the figure, again it stands that Isis bore him and Nephthys suckled him. In the Gospels the two appear in the persons of Anna and her daughter Mary. Anna gives birth to Mary; Mary gives birth to the Christ. Some scholars assert that Anna, the name, means simply "year," from Latin *annum,* "year." If by "year" is meant the annual round of nature's cycles, the origin may be credible. Mary in this case would be, not the Virgin Mother (that would be Anna, as the *first* or inorganic matter is the *virgin* form), but the Fish, or Spirit-Mother, and her son, born in Pisces, would testify to this character. However, it is only necessary to realize when ignorance followed intelligence, there was confusion in the precise handling of the symbols, and, as we have seen, both bread and fish symbols, as well as Virgo and Pisces features, have been combined and interblended.

IARU-TANA, ERIDANUS, JORDAN

The name given by the Hebrews to the stream of evolving life was of course the Jordan River, for they had named their one great river with that designation of the stream of evolution, taken from the sky charts of the earlier religious systems. The spelling of this name Jordan was derived from the name which the Greeks had given to it, the River Eridanus. And that, going back a step, was derived from the original name it bore in the Egyptian system, namely, the *Iaru-Tana. Iaru* is the Egyptian source of the Greek *hieros,* and of the Hebrew *Jeru* (in Jerusalem), both meaning "sacred," "divine." But *Tana* was actually the name of the geographical lake out of which the great Nile River had its source, the celestial lake of sea of source. It was localized in each country reformulating the archaic religious tradition to suit its geography as the main river or lake available on their map; in Egypt, the Nile, in Palestine the Jordan, in Babylonia and Persia the Tigris-Euphrates, in India the Indus or Ganges.

The fish as symbol must then be thought of as the system of organic material evolution that carries the nucleus of divine mind forward to its goal of the consummation of natural life in its final blossoming out into spiritual godhood. Whether discerned in its full spiritual significance or not, enough of this purport clings to the symbol in the primary motivations of Christianity to have been embodied in a feature of priestly attire, the Bishop's mitre, which is shaped in the form of the fish's mouth. The evidence for this is found in the Latin name of *os tincae,* or the tench's mouth, the tench being a fresh-water European fish, which, the dictionary says, was noted for its tenacity of life. The door of life was figured in the shape of a fish-mouth at the western, or feminine end of a church. The zodiacal Pisces is the house of the birth of Saviors; Jesus, Horus, Ioannes and other divine Avatars came as Ichthys, "fish" in Greek.

As has been seen, the fish's bladder denoted the presence of air in the water, and the stream of bubbles which one sees rising from the fish's mouth strengthens the suggestion as to the power of the natural world to generate and bring to the surface the power and function of mind (air) in the material conditions of physical life, symboled by water.

Vividly, then, the fish as symbol holds before our minds the idea that just as bubbles arise from the bottom of a pot of water when heat is applied beneath, so when the fire of divine spirit, through incarnation, is brought down under the watery elements in man's lower psychic nature, which are sense and emotion, the power of thought, reason, intelligence and understanding is generated and rises to the surface of consciousness exactly like the bubbles arising from the fish's mouth. Nature furnishes no end of these images of the forms of divine truth, but it seems we are too dull, blind and obtuse to discern them.

The fish symbol thus gives us the image of spirit-mind in submergence, or the god power buried in matter. In spite of its burial, however, it does not die, because it still can breathe under the water. Several chapter-titles of the *Book of the Dead* speak of "giving air to the soul of Nu in the underworld." Therefore ancient constructions of enlightened fancy, finding analogues ubiquitously in nature, pictured the god-soul in incarnation by the semainograph of the great fish transporting the divine unit of spirit through, across or under the sea of life and landing it safely on that "farther shore" of heavenly bliss and glory. Here is the core of all the meaning that could ever be attached to the Jonah-whale allegory. For, — do not doubt it — "Jonah," along with Joshua, Joses, Joash, Josiah, Jesse, Jehoash, Joram and others, is the same Jesus — and therefore conclusively allegorical — as he who in the New Testament was also tossed on a ship in the tempest, and, till aroused by the distressed sailors, was lying fast asleep in the lower part, or "belly" of the ship. This Jesus nature likewise lies long, all too long, asleep in the "hold" of the human ship, these "Red Sea" bodies of ours, until in the perils of the swirling tempests of our emotional and sensual life, he is aroused and bestirs himself to take the tiller of our barque in his hand of reason, conscience and his own divine impulsion, and allays the virulence of the storm by the strength of his mind and his will to righteousness.

The implications of the fish sign could be extended much further and some of them would yield rich essence of meaning. Enough has been presented here surely to indicate the graphic force of its suggestiveness for any reflecting mind. The central and cardinal significance is that of the analogue in the natural world of the living presence in the watery confines of the human body of the units of divine fiery essence of God-soul that can not be quenched even when submerged in the waters of the sea of life. The fish should be a trenchant reminder and assurance to us that even in the midst of the overflooding of our higher spiritual genius by the lower appetencies and the glamors of sense life, the fire of soul deep within us is unquenchable.

Not to be missed, also, is the emblemism of the mythic creature, the mermaid. The sign of Pisces does represent the feet of the human entity, as Aries, its neighbor the head. We have seen that the Eridanus River of life, emanating from the mouth of the Southern Fish, flowed right up to the foot of Orion. As the stellar type of the Christ in man, the star, or constellation of Orion is thus represented as standing in incarnation at the point where the upsurging stream of evolution of matter and form pours at his feet the forces and energies of the physical world, and it is for him to gather them up and utilize them. In this exertion and service he fulfills the purpose for which his heavenly Father sent him out to stand on the border between spirit and matter. So poetic imagery gave this creature of philosophical fancy, the mermaid, to typify man as the dual creature he is, combining the body of a natural animal with the soul of an embryonic god, in sea imagery a human with the feet or tail of the fish. It simply testifies with a charming figure that the base of man's life is immersed in the sea. The very throne of the great God Osiris was set over a symbolic tank of water. "The Lord sitteth upon the flood," says *Psalm* 29; and the majesty of *Psalm* 24 declares: "For he hath founded it upon the seas, and established it upon the floods." The Greek myth pictures Zeus as wading through the sea, and from the foam stirred up by the movement of his legs was born the Goddess of Love, Venus. Foam is a mixture of water and air and these spell emotion and mind. Love is the supreme blending of these two elements.

THE GREAT GREEN SEA.

It has been shown that the proper translation of the Hebrew *iam suph* as the Sea of Reeds, or Reed Sea, makes a drastic change in the great sea's color. The ancients sought for nature symbols in all directions. We do find it spoken of as the Emerald Sea. We are not surprised, then, to find that the Egyptians seers definitely poetized it as green from one line of metaphorical fancy, while from another image it is red. In the great *Ritual* of the Egyptian religion the supreme spiritual power, Ra, gives to Teta (one of the type names of the divine soul in man) "the power to journey over the Great Green Sea." Then it is said: "Thou sailest over the Lake of Kha, in the north of heaven, like a star passing over the Great Green Sea...as far as the place where is the star Seh (Orion)."

It has been elucidated above that the stream of life, Iaru-Tana(Eridanus, Jordan) issued from the mouth of the Southern Fish and flowed north to the feet of Orion, the Christ. So here again the star of soul, circuiting in its cycles the great sea of life, reaches at last this same star of Christhood, Orion, called by the Egyptians "the great star Seh."

But we need not go so far back as the Egyptians to find the imagery of this Great Sea, be its color red or green. In the fourth chapter of our *Book of Revelation* the metaphor presents this figure in resplendent glory indeed. "And before the throne there was a sea of glass like unto crystal." The "crystal sea" has ever been a symbol for spiritual mystics, hymnologists and rhapsodists to conjure with, as presenting some outward hint as to the pure radiancy of a more heavenly grade of consciousness than the one we normally experience on earth. And oddly enough, just as in the first chapter of *Genesis* this same river of life flowing forth from the throne of God divided into four heads, Gihon, Pison, Hiddekel and Euphrates, so here in *Revelation,* what is said immediately upon the statement of the presence of the crystal sea before the celestal throne is that "round about the throne were four beasts full of eyes before and behind." It turns out that these four "beasts," the lion, ox, man and eagle, represent four signs of the zodiac, Leo, Taurus, Aquarius and Scorpio; and these in turn represent sensation (earth), emotion (water), mind (air) and spirit (fire), the elements of the "vials of wrath" which the seven angels later pour out upon the world. How significant it is that "lo, in the midst of the throne and *of the four beasts* ... stood a Lamb, as it had been slain; having seven horns and seven eyes, which are the seven Spirits of God sent forth into all the earth." If we can visualize, if we can penetrate obvious outward symbolism to catch meaning in the conceptual world, we have here the picture of all that one needs to know, as the glyph and graph of the meaning of all sacred Scriptures. For we have the throne-power of God, the sea of glistening pure matter before it, the diffraction of God's creative power into seven rays of energy dispersion to activate the creation in space (with four of these energy forms bringing their products into visible manifestation, the other three still in the invisible world) and our own life manifesting the four grades of psychic consciousness, sensation, emotion, thought and spiritual will.

A most arresting detail of the picturization is that the clear glass of the crystal sea reflected the divine light of spirit which brooded over it. The watery field of life is pictured as a "crystal sea wherein the fire was reflected, and upon it there stood those who had overcome the influence of the Beast, who had not worshipped his image nor borne upon them the mark of his number." This reflection of the heavenly fire of divine spirit in the sea of life down here is most enchantingly intriguing. It is in complete accord with the main statement of the great Hermes, the mouthpiece allegedly of the body of the mighty Egyptian occult wisdom, when he says that "that which is above is as that which is below, and that which is below is as that which is above, for the performance of the miracle of the One Thing." Yes, nature, the lower world, the visible universe, reflects in its manifestations everywhere the creative forms, the archetypes of the divine Mind. Any body of still water reflects the heavens. "If thou wilt know the invisible," says Hermes, "open wide thine eyes on the visible."

The frequency with which the sea is mentioned in the Scriptures would indicate that it played an important part in the symbolism of the incarnation, as it obviously stood as a glyph for the human body blood. Some of these references to it in this meaning may be scrutinized. For instance, in *Exodus* 14:2, the Lord speaking to Moses, instructs him to tell the children of Israel that they "shall encamp by the sea." As these children of Israel are the hosts of his own Sons, whom he has sent to earth to live in immediate contact with this sea water of the animal bodies they must tenant here, the poetic expression of camping by the seaside would be quite felicitously apt to the situation. This will not appear at all strained or far-fetched when we consider that the great Jewish autumn festival of Succoth, tabernacles, booths or tents, in which they are ordered to live before they reach the Holy Land, are likewise a reference to the physical bodies in which they will be incarnate, as being a temporary and natural tenement for a temporary sojourn before they attain to their permanent spiritual bodies at the end of the incarnation series. For there is that spiritual "body of the resurrection" of which St. Paul speaks. The fleshly body is emblemed by more than one symbolic type in ancient allegorical depiction and in mythology, such as the well (of Beer-sheba), the cave (of Machpelah), the tomb, the pit, the prison, the desert and the wilderness.

Then it is said that the Egyptians overtook them as they encamped by the sea. Naturally this would be the case, as the Egyptians are the instincts, proclivities, habitudes and impulses of the bodily nature, and to say that they overtook the Israelites as they encamped by the sea is only poetically to say that these things caught them here in incarnation.

And most significantly appears in this same chapter the Lord's injunction to Moses, who is, of course, the figure of man spiritual, to "lift up thy rod and stretch out thine hand over the sea, and divide it," so that the Israelites would be able to walk through it on the dry ground, holding off the water. The "rod" in this drama is a definite symbol of man's inner soul power, his miracle-working force, and to stretch out the *hand* holding this rod over the sea was a vivid representation of man's developing and using his inner divine Self, in the exercise of which he is able to "subdue all things unto himself" and "put all things under his feet." The idea of the spiritual "fire" in man's nature drying out the moist nature and crossing a river or sea is very common in the ancient typology. The division of the sea into wet and dry portions would refer, by every inference, to the gradual separation of the soul and its interests from the first long subjection under the tyranny of the body and its instincts.

Very striking in its import can be the statement that the Israelites "came to Elim, where were twelve wells of water and three score and ten palm trees; and they encamped there by the waters." Universally the archaic Scriptures represented man's divinity as coming to full unfoldment through the development of twelve aspects or attributes of his Godhood; and the physical universe is actually founded on the number seven, as nature everywhere reveals. A ruse of the esotericists to hide occult truth from the "vulgar" masses was the adding of a meaningless cipher to the cardinal number, making the seven into seventy. The name Elim is composed of *el*, Hebrew for "God," and the masculine plural terminal *-im*. So the stage at which the Israelites became full-fledged gods is indicated by twelve wells of water and seven palm trees. As the palm is a product of hot tropical lands, it suggests the ubiquitous symbol of soul, namely, fire, branching out in seven rays.

The imagery employed by the Bible author indicates that the Lord raised up an east wind as his means for drying up the sea. The symbolism of east and west is too clear to be easily missed. The sun setting in the west was the nature-basis of souls sinking below the tim of the horizon of evolution into incarnation and, as it were, being immersed in the sea of life, under the picture of the sun setting in the ocean. In this state souls were overwhelmed in the body's watery life and nature and lived in what theology conceives to be "carnal sin." Passing around the cycle — represented by the six lower signs of the zodiac — they reach the point of rising above the horizon on the eastern side, and thus return to heaven, to spirit, to divine life. So the Egyptian *Book of the Dead* declares that Pepi — one of synonyms of the the human Ego-soul — "cometh into the eastern side of heaven, where the gods are born." The east, of course, carries all the intimations of the Easter resurrection of divine soul so long buried in the fleshly "body of this death," if we may use St. Paul's strong phrasing.

And so runs on the thrilling saga of the sea. It is understandable why the sapient sages of the past named the goddess Mothers after it, Thallath, Meri, Mary, Maya,

Miriam, Mylitta and the rest; for the sea is our universal Mother. We were all born out of her capacious bosom. And, being a true mother, her infinite care will abide with us forever.

When through the deep waters I call thee to go,
The rivers of woe shall not thee overflow;
For I will be with thee thy troubles to bless,
And sanctify to thee thy deepest distress.

"Deep calleth unto deep at the noise of thy waterspouts: all thy waves and thy billows are gone over me."

"For thou hadst cast me into the deep, in the midst of the seas; and the floods encompassed me about; all thy billows and thy waves passed over me. The waters compassed me about, even to the soul; the depth closed me round about, the weeds were wrapped about my head. I went down to the bottom of the mountains; the earth with her bars was about me for ever; yet hast thou brought up my life from corruption, O Lord my God."

"The sea is his, and he made it."

The Sea is his and he made it. *Psalm 95.*

And all the waters that were in the river were turned to blood. *Exodus 7:20.*

And the water which thou takest out of the river shall become blood upon the dry land. *Exodus 4:9.*